Knickerbocker Number Nine

Poems chosen by
Richard Brown and Kate Ruttle

Illustrated by
John Bendall-Brunello
and Sarah McDonald

CAMBRIDGE
UNIVERSITY PRESS

Cambridge Reading

General Editors
Richard Brown and Kate Ruttle

Consultant Editor
Jean Glasberg

PUBLISHED BY THE PRESS SYNDICATE OF THE UNIVERSITY OF CAMBRIDGE
The Pitt Building, Trumpington Street, Cambridge CB2 1RP

CAMBRIDGE UNIVERSITY PRESS
The Edinburgh Building, Cambridge CB2 2RU, United Kingdom
40 West 20th Street, New York, NY 10011-4211, USA
10 Stamford Road, Oakleigh, Melbourne 3166, Australia

Knickerbocker Number Nine
This selection © Richard Brown and Kate Ruttle 1996
Illustrations © John Bendall-Brunello and Sarah McDonald 1996

First published 1996
Reprinted 1998

Typeset in Concorde

Printed in the United Kingdom at the University Press, Cambridge

A catalogue record for this book is available from the British Library

ISBN 0 521 49994 1 paperback

Contents

What I Like   *Tony Bradman*   4

Skipping Rhymes   *Anon*   6

Slide   *Sheila Simmons*   7

Muddy Puddle   *Dennis Lee*   8

The Soil in the Garden   *Joan Poulson*   10

Jacks   *Tony Bradman*   12

Three-Hole   *John Agard*   14

Doctor Knickerbocker   *Anon*   16

Annie, Annie   *Beverly McLoughland*   18

The Shadow Tree   *Ilo Orleans*   19

Wings   *Pie Corbett*   20

Playing with Words   *Michael Rosen*   22

Reading   *Marchette Chute*   23

Index of first lines   24

What I Like

I like watching telly,
I like to have fun,
I like playing outside
And I love to run.

But there's one thing I love,
That I really adore –
I love reading books
And I've got to have more!

I like eating lollies
And hate them to end,
I like doing nothing
When I'm with my friends.

But there's something so gripping,
There's something I need,
In a really good book
That I've just got to read.

I like being awkward,
And I love to laugh,
I love eating burgers
And hate having baths.

But here's one thing that's greater,
Come inside, take a look;
There's nothing quite like
A really good book!

Tony Bradman

Skipping Rhymes

What's your name?
Johnny Maclean.
Where do you live?
Down the lane.

What's your shop?
Lollipop.
What's your number?
Cucumber.

What's your name?
Mary Jane.
Where do you live?
Cabbage Lane.
What's your number?
Rain and thunder.
What address?
Watercress.

Anon

Slide

I count aloud
as I clang up the steps
to the top of the slide
in the park.

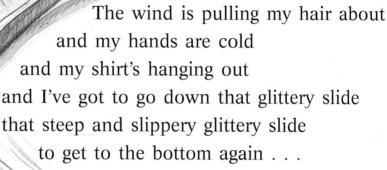

The wind is pulling my hair about
and my hands are cold
and my shirt's hanging out
and I've got to go down that glittery slide
that steep and slippery glittery slide
to get to the bottom again . . .
So . . .
I close my eyes . . .
let go . . .
and whoosh . . .

I swoop . . .
like a diving plane!
Off with a jump,
back to the steps
and up to the top again!

Sheila Simmons

Muddy Puddle

I am sitting
In the middle
Of a rather Muddy
Puddle,
With my bottom
Full of bubbles
And my rubbers
Full of Mud,

While my jacket
And my sweater
Go on slowly
Getting wetter
As I very
Slowly settle
To the Bottom
Of the Mud.

And I find that
What a person
With a puddle
Round his middle
Thinks of mostly
In the muddle
Is the Muddi-
Ness of Mud.

Dennis Lee

The Soil in the Garden

The soil in the garden
is dry and crumbly.
I rub it in my fingers
and let it dribble slowly,
make a squiggly pattern
curvy-looped and swirly,
then BLOW!
and it flies, like a
dancer, light and twirly.

The soil in the garden
is wet and heavy.
I rub it in my fingers
and feel it muddy-sticky,
make a floppy pancake
squodgy, sloppy-sticky,
then CLAP!
and it splatters, like a
shower, freckly-flicky.

Joan Poulson

Jacks

Five silver jacks,
One rubber ball,
A playground game
For one and all.

Throw the ball,
Pick up one,
Now our game
Has just begun.

Throw the ball,
Pick up two,
One for me
And one for you.

Throw the ball,
Pick up . . . three!
One for you
And two for me.

Throw the ball . . .
Pick up . . . four!
Whoops! I've dropped
One on the floor.

Throw the ball,
Here I go,
I'll try for five –
Can I? No!

Throw the ball,
Try again . . .
I've got all five!
I could do TEN!

Five silver jacks,
All in a row . . .
Here, take the ball –
Would you like a go?

Tony Bradman

Three-Hole

Three-hole
is the name
of a marble game
we got in Guyana.

Is fun to play
and not hard.
Just dig three lil holes
in you yard
or the sand
by you gate.
Then aim straight

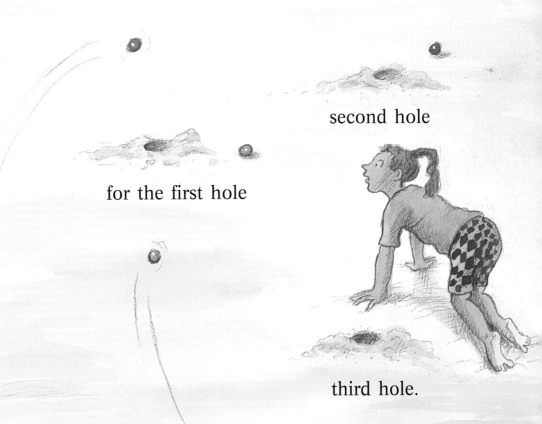

for the first hole

second hole

third hole.

If you lucky
and you marble
go in all the holes
one two three

Then is you chance
to knock you friend marble.
Send it flying for a dance.
When marble burst then fun start.

John Agard

Doctor Knickerbocker

Doctor Knickerbocker,
Knickerbocker number nine,
Loves to dance to the rhythm of time.
Now let's get the rhythm of the hands
    CLAP CLAP
Now we've got the rhythm of the hands
    CLAP CLAP
Now let's get the rhythm of the feet
    STAMP STAMP
Now we've got the rhythm of the feet
    STAMP STAMP

Now let's get the rhythm of the eyes
WIPE WIPE
Now we've got the rhythm of the eyes
WIPE WIPE
Now let's get the rhythm of the dance
WIGGLE WIGGLE
Now we've got the rhythm of the dance
WIGGLE WIGGLE
CLAP CLAP,
STAMP STAMP,
WIPE WIPE,
WIGGLE WIGGLE
Now we're dancing to the rhythm of time,
Doctor Knickerbocker,
Knickerbocker number nine.

Anon

Annie, Annie

Annie, Annie
Climbing trees,
Scrapes her elbows,
Skins her knees,
Scuffs her shoes
And snags her hair —
What's Annie doing
Way up there?

Annie, Annie
Says it's fun
Climbing closer
To the sun,
Far up where
It's grand to be
As high as high
And swinging free.

Beverly McLoughland

The Shadow Tree

I'd love to sit
On the highest branch
But it's much too high
For me;

So I sit in the grass
Where the shadow falls,
On the top of
The shadow tree.

Ilo Orleans

Wings

If I had wings
   I would touch the fingertips of clouds
     and glide on the wind's breath.

     If I had wings
        I would taste a chunk of the sun,
           as hot as peppered curry.

    If I had wings
      I would listen to the clouds of sheep bleat
        that graze on the blue.

If I had wings
   I would breathe deep and sniff
     the scent of raindrops.

If I had wings
  I would gaze at the people
    who cling to the earth.

If I had wings
  I would dream of
    swimming the deserts
    and walking the seas.

Pie Corbett

Playing with Words

You can play with dice
You can play with cards
You can play with a ball
You can play with words
       words
       words
       words
       words
       words
       words
       banana
       words
       words
       words
       words
       words

Michael Rosen

Reading

A story is a special thing.
The ones that I have read,
They do not stay inside the book,
They stay inside my head.

Marchette Chute

Index of first lines

A story is a special thing   23

Annie, Annie   18

Doctor Knickerbocker   16

Five silver jacks   12

I am sitting   8

I count aloud   7

I like watching telly   4

I'd love to sit   19

If I had wings   21

The soil in the garden   10

Three-hole   14

What's your name?   6

You can play with dice   22